MW01075982

Examination
of Conscience
Guided *by the*
Holy Spirit

DAVID KNIGHT

TWENTY-THIRD
PUBLICATIONS
twentythirdpublications.com

Twenty-Third Publications
One Montauk Avenue, Suite 200
New London, CT 06320
(860) 437-3012 or (800) 321-0411
www.twentythirdpublications.com

ISBN: 978-1-62785-666-9
Cover image: fr_Kosma/Shutterstock.com
Printed in the U.S.A.

 A division of Bayard, Inc.

CONTENTS

INTRODUCTION

What does it really mean to be a Christian?

If we are living authentic Christian lives, we should be the "aroma of Christ" in the world. That is, wherever we are, whatever we do and say, people should feel in our presence what they felt in the presence of Jesus.

Paul says that through us Jesus "spreads in every place the fragrance that comes from knowing him. For we are the aroma of Christ" (2 Corinthians 2:14–17). If we are not the "aroma of Christ," we are not living authentically Christian lives, no matter how perfectly we keep the Ten Commandments or how frequently we plunk our bodies in the pews. How do we know whether we are the aroma of Christ? It is simple. We ask whether the "fruit of the Spirit" is evident in our lives.

When we evaluate our lives as Christians, we should not begin by looking for our "sins." Our first question should be, Is the fruit of the Spirit visible in my life? Do people see me, above all, as loving? Do they sense a deep, underlying joy in me, even when things are not going well? Do I give the impression of being at peace with myself and seeking peace with everyone around me? "The fruit of the Spirit is Love, Joy, Peace…."

We are not talking here about ordinary human virtues. These are not just character traits deliberately developed or culturally acquired. Human efforts play a part, of course, but they cannot explain the end product. To be a Christian is to be divine. If the fruits of the Spirit are evident in our life, we will be the "aroma of Christ" in the world. And for the world.

Come, Holy Spirit, fill the hearts of your faithful.

And kindle in us the fire of your divine love. Send forth your Spirit, Lord, and our hearts will be regenerated. And you will renew the face of the earth! God, by the light of the Holy Spirit, you instruct the hearts of your faithful:

Grant us by the Gifts of Wisdom,
Understanding, Knowledge,
Counsel, Family Spirit, Strength,
and Awe of the Lord that we may
not be conformed to this world but
transformed by the renewal of our
minds, so that we might discern
and do what is good, acceptable,
and pleasing to you, and perfect;

And so be the aroma of Christ
in the world through Love,
Joy, Peace, Patient Endurance,
Kindness, Generosity, Faithfulness,
Gentleness, and the Self-Control of
total surrender to your Spirit.

The
FRUIT
of LOVE

On a day-to-day basis,
how do I show
the fruit of love?

"As the Father has loved me, so I have loved you; abide in my love....This is my commandment, that you love one another as I have loved you." **JOHN 15:9, 12**

When I wake up in the morning, do I remind myself that I am getting up to love?

Do I know that God loves me? Do I understand why?

Do I discriminate against anyone? Treat anyone as less important than anyone else? Do I show the same respect to the janitor that I show to my boss?

Do I fulfill all of my religious obligations, not as "obligations" but as loving, personal responses to Jesus and to the Father, in conscious union with the Holy Spirit?

The
FRUIT
of JOY

On a day-to-day basis,
how do I show
the fruit of joy?

*"I have told you this so that my joy might
be in you and your joy might be complete."*
JOHN 15:11

Would most people who know me call me
a joyful person?

Aside from temporary disturbances, is there
anything deep and abiding that diminishes
my joy?

Do I know how to find joy in Christ when
there is suffering in my life? When I am
frustrated?

If I made a list of the things that take
away my joy, could I match each one
with something from the gospels
that gives me joy in spite of them?

The
FRUIT *of* PEACE

On a day-to-day basis,
how do I show
the fruit of peace?

*"Peace I give to you…Do not let your hearts
be troubled, and do not let them be afraid."*
JOHN 14:27

Do I have an abiding peace in my heart?

Where is my "anchor hold"—the place
where I can go to find peace? How often do
I use it?

Am I "worried and distracted by many
things"? Have I consciously, personally,
decided "there is need of only one thing"
(see Luke 10:42)? What is that?

When I know I am right and others
are wrong, am I more inclined to seek
common ground through dialogue or to
prove my point through argument?

The

FRUIT *of* PATIENT ENDURANCE

On a day-to-day basis,
how do I show the fruit
of patient endurance?

The LORD, the LORD, a God gracious and merciful, slow to anger and abounding in love and fidelity.... **EXODUS 34:6**

Do I see that the key to patient endurance is responding with positive acts of kindness to annoyances, insults, or injustices?

Do I cultivate "an abiding inclination to be of assistance" in action?

When someone does wrong, is my first reaction concern for the wrongdoer, as it would be for one of my children, or is it to see justice done? Do I want justice with mercy, or simply justice?

Do I understand Pope Francis's warning: "Being patient does not mean letting ourselves be constantly mistreated, tolerating physical aggression, or allowing other people to use us"?

The
FRUIT *of*
KINDNESS

**On a day-to-day basis,
how do I show the fruit
of kindness?**

God, who is rich in mercy…loved us even when we were dead…so that…God might show…God's…kindness toward us in Christ Jesus. **EPHESIANS 2:4–7**

Do I get up in the morning to spend my day being kind to others?

Throughout the day, do I keep my focus on what I can do for others, instead of on what others are doing to me, or not doing for me?

When anyone wrongs me, imposes on me, or annoys me in any way, is my immediate reaction to "be of assistance" by doing something kind?

Do I agree that the divine Kindness that is a fruit of the Spirit is kindness to everyone, but above all to those who do not deserve it?

The
FRUIT *of*
GENEROSITY

**On a day-to-day basis,
how do I show the fruit
of patient generosity?**

"If anyone wants to sue you and take your coat, give your cloak as well." **MATTHEW 5:40**

Is my first priority in life relationship? Cultivating relationship with God and other human persons?

Do I consciously deal with everyone the way I would with my brother or sister?

Do I refuse to break off my relationship with anyone because of a concern about money or possessions? Rather than lose (an authentic) relationship, do I prefer to give to others whatever they want—even more than they ask? Do I do it with unexpected generosity?

When people I live and work with make my job harder or longer by not doing the things they should, do I respond with a generosity that shows I value relationship with them more than my time?

The

FRUIT *of*
FAITHFULNESS

On a day-to-day basis,
how do I show the fruit
of patient faithfulness?

I was overjoyed when some of the friends arrived and testified to your faithfulness to the truth, namely how you walk in the truth.
3 JOHN 3

Do I believe I can actually be "friends" with the infinite, transcendent God who is Being Itself? What makes that kind of relationship with God possible? Am I doing what it takes?

What in my life makes it visibly evident that my religion is a religion of relationship rather than a religion of rules?

What concrete actions or choices in my life show that my religion is a religion that seeks relationship with God, and others?

What do I do just to know God better?

The
FRUIT *of*
GENTLENESS

On a day-to-day basis,
how do I show the fruit
of patient gentleness?

"Come to me, all you that are weary and are carrying heavy burdens, and I will give you rest. Take my yoke upon you and learn from me; for I am gentle and humble in heart, and you will find rest for your souls."

MATTHEW 11:28–29

Would those who know me best say I am "gentle and humble of heart"? What do I do that would make them say it or not say it?

Does my attitude, my "aura," my way of dealing with people, proclaim the Good News that our God is a gentle God?

Do I believe that in the measure we reject the way of Gentleness in favor of force, violence, and power, we actually reject Jesus?

When persuasion doesn't work, do I ever use power? Choose force over Gentleness?

The
FRUIT *of*
SELF-
CONTROL

On a day-to-day basis,
how do I show the fruit
of patient self-control?

You must make every effort to support your faith with goodness…knowledge…self-control… endurance…godliness…mutual affection, and…love. For…they keep you from being ineffective and unfruitful in the knowledge of our Lord Jesus Christ. 2 PETER 1:5-8

In my life, how do I try to exercise control over myself? Over others? Over things I am involved in?

In each of my answers to the questions above, when is my control surrender to God, and when is it just self-assertion?

Does the way I live my faith give me a sense of security based on my behavior? Does it make me feel superior to others when I "observe certain rules or remain intransigently faithful to a particular Christian style from the past"?

Deep down, do I really trust God to do everything Jesus promises?

The
FRUIT *of*
COMMUNAL
PEACE

On a day-to-day basis,
how do I show the fruit
of patient communal peace?

"The glory that you have given me I have given them, so that they may be One, as we are One, I in them and you in me, that they may become completely One, so that the world may know that you have sent me and have loved them even as you have loved me."

JOHN 17:22–23

What does visible, conscious, personal relationship with Jesus have to do with Christians' experience of their relationship with each other?

Do you recognize people who, regardless of their professed religion, or lack of it, seem to be listening to the Holy Spirit?

What is your reaction to change and to people who call for changes? Do you dialogue? Listen? Voice answers to questions and challenges? Seek more information about what is new to you?

For you, what is the difference in a Christian community between uniformity and harmony?

When there is a problem, do you dialogue with respect, believing that the other person has something good to say?

Would you say that in your parish or diocese there are visible efforts to establish what Francis calls "the culture of dialogue, the culture of encounter"?

How do you see your parish drawing people to the Church today as in the beginning, when "day by day the Lord added to their number those who were being saved"?

When and how do you see the Christian community giving expression, in physical words and gestures, to the invisible faith, hope, and love in our minds and wills and hearts?

To see whether you are living the Life of God or not, check to see whether the fruit of the Spirit is visible in your life. By your fruit you will know what you are (see Matthew 7:16; Luke 6:43). Let this booklet be a new beginning for you. Live "life to the full." Live on the level of God.

And the peace of God, which surpasses all understanding, will guard your hearts and your minds in Christ Jesus.

PHILIPPIANS 4:7

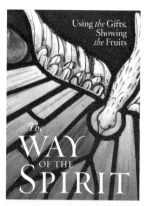